With love for our son Sammy and our daughter Becky

Our experience of Autism is living every day with the unexpected:
joy, pride for achievements and the challenges of living with autism.
This book illustrates in simple terms how autism, particularly
sensory perception, can impact on the behaviour of children.

Thanks to everyone who tries to help and understand Sammy.

ISBN: 978-1-5032-3009-5

Why Does Sammy Do That?

Written by Melanie Janz

Illustrated by Ezra Allen

Everyone is different
Some people are tall, some are small.
Some people are big, some very slim.

Some people have brown hair with lots of curls in it.
Some have blond, red, black or even blue hair.
Everyone looks different on the outside.

But inside we all have a heart that beats
and pumps blood through the body so we can live.
We all have a wonderful brain in our heads.

The brain is a place where you can have the most wonderful
adventures, where you can remember your very best day
and where you learn and explore the world.

But sometimes the brain does strange things.
Sammy is a wonderful boy with autism.
Autism means Sammy's brain does strange things.

When your ears hear a loud bang, your brain tells you "That was loud!"
But Sammy's brain tells him " That is fun, I want more!"
So he bangs the door.

When your nose smells the soap on the freshly
 washed clothes, your brain tells you
" Mmmh, that smells good."

But Sammy's brain tells him "Yuk disgusting!"
So he pulls the washing off the line.

When your tongue tastes the sweetness and sandiness of a pear, your brain tells you "Yummy delicious, I want more."

But Sammy's brain tells him "Yuk horrible" and he spits out the pear and screams.

When somebody stands behind you and touches
 your back, your brain tells you
 " I can feel something. Look around and see who's there"

But Sammy's brain tells him "Ouch that hurts me terribly" and Sammy starts to scream.

When you push a toy car along,
your brain tells you " That's a fun game. Let's play car race!"

But Sammy's brain tells him
"Wow the wheels go round and round.
Let me see this again and again!"
and Sammy will push the car for a very long time.

When you play knights in a castle, and another child wants to be in your castle too,
your brain tells you "Great, let's play together!"

But Sammy's brain tells him
"Oh no! There is somebody blocking my way into the castle. HELP!"
And Sammy pushes the other child away or screams and tries to bite.

When you sit or stand anywhere, your brain tells you "This is up, this is down. I know where I am in the room."

But Sammy's brain says " I don't know where I am in the room. Jump to find out!" So Sammy jumps wildly on the sofa.

When you like somebody and want to play with them, your brain tells you
"I want to be their friend. Ask to be their friend!"

But Sammy's brain says
" ⚡ ⚒ 🚫 🚌 ☹ 💥 💣 ✳ ✖ ❓ !!&?? AAHHH!

I don't know what it means to be a friend."
Sammy looks confused and plays alone.

But the brain is a wonderful place for learning new things.
So with your help, understanding and lots of nice smiles,

We all might learn from each other and have fun together.

So, we all look different on the outside.
Some people also are different on the inside.

But we all look the same when we smile at one another.

Made in the USA
Lexington, KY
07 May 2019